SHIPWRECKS

BY

DAVID & SUSAN SPENCE

THE DIVING BARREL

An early and crude mechanically assisted piece of diving apparatus was Jacob Rowe's diving barrel, invented in 1753. The diver was encased in a hollow copper vessel with two holes for the occupant's arms to protrude and a glass window at one end. This enabled the diver to stay under the water for up to 30 minutes until all the air inside had been used up.

Exploring the Deep

Ships have been wrecked for as long as man has gone to sea. Some of the earliest evidence we have of ancient civilizations has come from wrecked ships. These are often time capsules carrying valuable information about the way the ships were built, the crews that sailed them, and the passengers and cargoes they carried. This evidence enables researchers to build a vivid picture of the society of the time. Today, sophisticated technology enables us to investigate deeper under the waves so that vessels such as the *Titanic* are beginning to yield their secrets.

THE DIVING BELL

The principle of the diving bell, which allowed a person to be submerged while breathing air through a tube from the surface, has been known about and tried since at least the time of Aristotle (*c.* 350 B.C.). In the early 18th century Halley produced a crude diving bell made of wood and coated in lead to make it heavy enough to sink. This was bell-shaped with a top of clear glass to provide light and a device to let out air expended by its user. The bell was reported to have been used at a depth of 60 feet (18 meters).

THE DIVING SUIT

A flexible suit was invented in 1797 by C.H. Klingert. It was made of tinplate and watertight leather and allowed the diver to walk around on the seabed. Air was supplied through tubes from the ship above.

THE UNDERWATER LUNG

It wasn't until 1943, with the invention of the aqualung by, among others, Jacques Yves Cousteau, that modern-day exploration greatly progressed. An air-regulating device, used in wartime gas-driven car engines, was adapted for use with the Le Prieur diving apparatus. The aqualung automatically provided air to the diver from bottles strapped to the back. Divers were now free from all the heavy diving gear they had previously had to put up with.

THE ARMORED SUIT

The most modern diving suits, called hardsuits, are armored and capable of withstanding the incredible water pressure from outside, which builds up the deeper the diver goes. Literally tons of water above the diver's head generate enormous water pressure, so the suit needs to maintain tolerable air pressure inside at depths of up to 1,180 feet (360 meters). The designs are based on early suits of armor, which found ways of jointing arms and legs, permitting the wearer freedom of movement.

SEARCHING THE WRECKS

Diving on wrecks is a popular pastime as well as a serious venture. With the aid of the wetsuit and aqualung, many enthusiasts around the world search out the treasures of the deep.

The Hazards of the Sea

ICEBERGS

Icebergs are floating masses of frozen freshwater that have broken free from an ice sheet. They are most common in spring months when the warmer weather melts the Greenland and Antarctic ice shelves. Icebergs can be small lumps of ice or huge blocks the size of a ten-story building. Only one-seventh is visible above the waterline. Small icebergs, known as growlers, are difficult to detect on a ship's sonar.

Ships face many dangers on the open seas. Storms, fog, and underwater reefs are as dangerous today as they ever were, but technology today gives the vigilant crew more advanced warning than their predecessors ever had. Accurate weather forecasting and ship-to-shore communication mean that vessels are able to take precautions when storms approach, either sheltering in harbor or taking alternate routes. All seagoing ships now carry global positioning systems (GPS) that use satellite technology to fix their position with pinpoint accuracy, and similarly advanced equipment determines how much clearance there is between the ship's hull and the seabed at all times. Most of the world's coastline is mapped, and detailed charts, together with local pilots, help the ship's crew to navigate successfully without incident. But the age-old hazards of the sea still remain.

CORAL REEFS

Reefs are ridges of rock, sand, or coral that lie close to the surface of the sea. Ships risk running aground on these ridges, which can cause fatal damage to the hull or just hold the ship fast. Hard coral reefs grow extremely slowly, so reefs damaged by ships may take hundreds of years to recover.

HURRICANES

The hurricane season, between June and December, is particularly dangerous to shipping in the danger areas of the Caribbean and Gulf of Mexico, where the average sea temperature of 80° F (27°C) produces water vapor that fuels the strong winds. The hurricane's wall of cloud is pushed by winds that can reach over 150 mph (240 km/h). At their center is the "eye" of the hurricane, a calm area measuring about 20 miles (32 km) in diameter.

WHALE ALERT!

Large humpback whales used to pose a danger to shipping – they could unwittingly overturn a sailing ship because of their sheer size. Today the ships are much bigger than the whales and the dangers are reversed. Supertankers and big cargo vessels can literally "run over" whales while they lie sleeping in the water. Some enlightened companies are now developing electronic whale alarms to wake the whales, so they have time to swim to safety.

STORMS

Bad storms at sea have been a common curse for sailors over the centuries. Here the fishermen of a sinking trawler are being rescued in the storm-tossed North Sea.

FOG AND ROCKS

Ships have long relied on lighthouses to warn them of danger at sea, particularly around rocky coasts. The most famous lighthouse is the Pharos of Alexandria, one of the Seven Wonders of the World, which was built around 280 B.C. The first lighthouses used coal fires, which were then replaced with oil lamps and, finally, electric lamps.

THE RESTORED SHIP

The timbers of the wreck were brought to the surface and treated over a period of time with polyethylene glycol, which preserves the wood. The pieces were then reassembled at the Bodrum Museum, specially built by the Turkish government. The ship was found to be similar in construction to the Egyptian vessels of the time, with a relatively flat bottom, steep sides and hardly any keel, making it easy to navigate in shallow waters, but unsuitable for open seas. The evidence of the retrieved timbers shows how the shipwrights had developed a method of planking over frames, which determined the hull shape, instead of fixing planking before building a frame, as was common practice in the Mediterranean before the date of the wreck.

THE GLASS JIGSAW PUZZLE

Hundreds of thousands of pieces of broken glass were recovered by the archaeologists, who estimate that they once made up some 10–20,000 glass vessels. Two hundred of these vessels, such as bottles and jugs, have been painstakingly pieced together in a giant glass jigsaw puzzle.

UNDERWATER ARCHAEOLOGY

The wide range of glass goods, including jugs, jars, bottles, bowls, and cups, appear to have been made in Syria and show signs of Islamic patterned molds. The ship was also carrying Islamic glazed bowls, decorated with splash-ware (colored glazes splashed onto the interior surface), as well as sgraffito-ware (designs carved into the surface of the clay). Archaeologists also discovered 104 amphoras (round clay pots with narrow necks), most of which had been used for wine or olive oil.

The Glass Puzzle

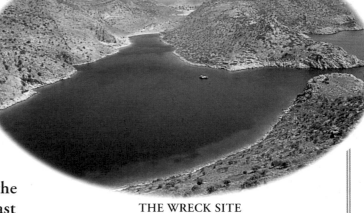

THE WRECK SITE

The wreck was located at the harbor of Serce Limani on the southern coast of Turkey, opposite the Greek island of Rhodes.

In 1977 members of the Institute of Nautical Archaeology started to excavate the wreck of the *Serce Limani,* which was located 108 ft. (33 m) under the sea off the southern coast of Turkey. Large amounts of broken glass were seen littered around the wreck site. Divers mapped the area by placing a square metal frame over the remains, searching and recording the contents of the frame, then moving the frame, thereby gradually building up a grid pattern over the whole site. The location of every object was meticulously recorded in this way. Archaeologists slowly built up a picture of a small two-masted lateen rigged ship, approximately 49 ft. (15 m) long, dating from the 11th century. It became clear that it was a cargo ship that was carrying a range of goods for trading. This included wine, raisins, bowls, glassware, and three tons of raw glass in small pieces, which would have been used to manufacture glassware. It is likely that the ship was on its way to Constantinople (now Istanbul), the most important city at that time and a producer of Byzantine glassware.

LIFE IN THE 11TH CENTURY

The ship is a time capsule that helps historians understand life of the period. This filigree gold earring was probably carried as bullion along with a few other items of jewelry and some coins. Three lead seals used for documents were discovered. This suggests that the ship may have been carrying letters of credit rather than risk losing valuables to pirates. Other items give a fascinating insight into 11th-century life, such as the chess set and backgammon pieces recovered from the living quarters, as well as other personal belongings such as a wooden comb and scissors.

The *Mary Rose*

One of the most famous shipwrecks is the *Mary Rose*, flagship of Henry VIII's fleet, which sank at Spithead off Portsmouth in 1545 with the loss of 500 lives. She carried valuable armory, so attempts at salvaging the ship were immediately planned. Efforts proved fruitless and were abandoned, but in 1836 the Deane brothers rediscovered the wreck, using the diving helmet invented by John Deane. After the initial excitement, the wreck was again left until it was rediscovered in 1967, using modern sonar equipment. A *Mary Rose* committee was set up to try to gain legal protection for the wreck and six years later, in 1973, England passed the "Protection of Wreck" Act. By 1979 the Mary Rose Trust had been established, with the aim of raising the wreck and establishing a museum in Portsmouth, England. This was finally achieved in 1982.

DOWN SHE GOES

The Imperial English Ambassador reported that the French fleet came into view while Henry VIII was at dinner on the flagship. He went ashore and the English fleet was attacked by five French galleys.

The *Mary Rose* sank towards evening. A survivor's report suggested that when she leaned over, water entered the lowest row of gunports, which had remained open after firing. The brother of the Vice Admiral reported that she began to heel as soon as the sails were raised. When asked what was wrong, Vice Admiral Sir George Carew said *"that in his ships a hundred mariners, the worst of them being able to be a master in the best ship in the realm; and these so maligned and disdained one another, that refusing to do that which they should do, were careless to do that which was most needful and necessary."* It seems that she sank because of bad seamanship, possibly while attempting to do too tight a turn, which dipped her open gunports into the sea.

THE *MARY ROSE* RECOVERED

Archaeologists and engineers devised a plan to raise the ship from its resting place on the seabed by means of steel cradles that were hoisted to the surface. The wreck is now at Portsmouth Dockyard in England and attracts thousands of visitors each year.

BABCOCK POWER CONSTRUCTION DIVISION

ALL HUMAN LIFE

The *Mary Rose* was a living picture of Tudor life when she sank. Found on the wreck in the officers quarters were musical instruments, a pewter jug, gold coins, and smooth, well-turned bowls. In other parts of the ship were found more roughly turned wooden tableware, nit combs, a simple gaming board, bows and arrows, crossbow bolts, planes, sheathed knives, leather clothing, rope, barrels of tar, lanterns, rigging blocks, firewood, and sailcloth. The crew appeared to be well nourished. This may have been due to the fact that they only fought across narrow seas, so fresh supplies were always available.

FROM CLINKER TO CARAVEL

In 1536, the *Mary Rose* was completely rebuilt in the more modern "caravel" fashion similar to Mediterranean ships of the period. Caravels were built with the planks laid flush with each other. This enabled square gunports to be cut in the hull with efficient watertight seals that could be lowered and tightly closed. This design meant that the guns could be brought down within the hull, lowering the center of gravity, and permitting two rows of gunports instead of the normal one row.

HENRY VIII

Throughout Henry VIII's rule he had battled on and off with Francis I of France. On Sunday, July 19 1545, the *Mary Rose*, pride of Henry VIII's fleet, sank as he watched horrified from the nearby shore. Contemporary reports of the event differ. An engraving of the time shows that few, if any, of the ships had set sail, suggesting little wind, and that they were leaving Portsmouth at high water on an ebb tide. French reports stated that at dawn on a calm sea their galleys started battle, trying to lure the English towards their main fleet.

THE BATTLE RAGES

When the Spanish Armada came into view up the English Channel, the English fleet set sail from Plymouth ready to engage in battle. Battles were fought off Plymouth, Portland, and the Isle of Wight.

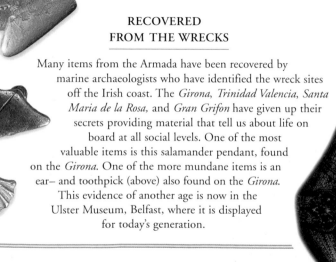

RECOVERED
FROM THE WRECKS

Many items from the Armada have been recovered by marine archaeologists who have identified the wreck sites off the Irish coast. The *Girona, Trinidad Valencia, Santa Maria de la Rosa,* and *Gran Grifon* have given up their secrets providing material that tell us about life on board at all social levels. One of the most valuable items is this salamander pendant, found on the *Girona*. One of the more mundane items is an ear– and toothpick (above) also found on the *Girona*. This evidence of another age is now in the Ulster Museum, Belfast, where it is displayed for today's generation.

The Spanish Armada

By the mid-16th century Catholic Spain and France were both struggling for supremacy in Europe. In the 1580s England's Protestant Queen, Elizabeth I, became determined "that the King of Spain's greatness should be impeached." In 1587 England directly challenged Spanish sovereignty in the Netherlands. King Philip II of Spain prepared for battle. He warned his captains that the English had faster ships and, because of their longer range guns, would try to avoid fighting at close quarters. He left the order of battle to his captains. The Great Armada (or "most happy fleet") set sail from Lisbon in the new year of 1588 with 130 ships and over 30,000 men ready to invade England. After a number of battles, the English sent in fire ships while the Armada lay anchored at Calais, causing the fleet to scatter and break up its formation. The Spanish were never to recover and decided to retreat to Spain.

A TREACHEROUS JOURNEY

This chart shows the track of the Armada around the British coastline. It encountered terrible weather including freezing fog and storms on its homeward journey. Between August 21 and September 3, 17 ships had disappeared during night storms as the ships were driven onto the Irish coastline by fierce winds. Those fortunate enough to reach dry land were captured and executed.

The English considered this harsh treatment at the hands of the elements "divine retribution" against the Spanish— clearly God was on their side. In all as many as 11,000 men perished, most drowning as their ships failed to withstand the pounding seas.

ROYAL RIVALS

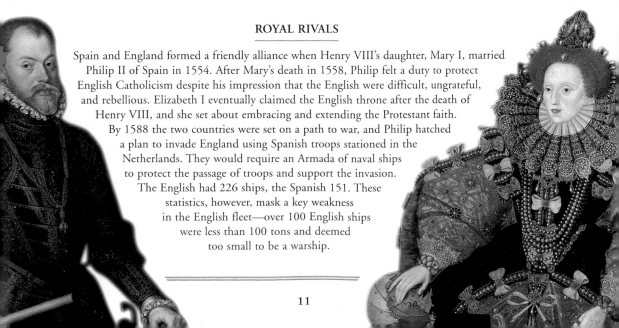

Spain and England formed a friendly alliance when Henry VIII's daughter, Mary I, married Philip II of Spain in 1554. After Mary's death in 1558, Philip felt a duty to protect English Catholicism despite his impression that the English were difficult, ungrateful, and rebellious. Elizabeth I eventually claimed the English throne after the death of Henry VIII, and she set about embracing and extending the Protestant faith. By 1588 the two countries were set on a path to war, and Philip hatched a plan to invade England using Spanish troops stationed in the Netherlands. They would require an Armada of naval ships to protect the passage of troops and support the invasion. The English had 226 ships, the Spanish 151. These statistics, however, mask a key weakness in the English fleet—over 100 English ships were less than 100 tons and deemed too small to be a warship.

Spanish Gold

During the 16th and 17th centuries, European states expanded their empires overseas. In 1492 Christopher Columbus claimed the "New World" of the central Americas for Spain. These lands were known as the "Spanish Main" and Spain looted the rich treasures found there, shipping them back home. The richest booty came from the Aztec peoples of Mexico and the Inca tribes of Peru, who produced vast quantities of silver and gold, as well as many precious stones. The New Americas were enormously wealthy and both the English and the French wanted to gain a foothold. They greatly resented the Spanish, who fiercely defended their monopoly. At first, privateers (armed vessels commissioned by government) were employed to attack the treasure laden Spanish ships, and many were sunk in and around the Caribbean. Francis Drake was to be one such privateer, at first incurring the wrath of Elizabeth I, then receiving her backing, and eventually becoming knighted.

ATOCHA TREASURE

Gold was a much-prized treasure. Francis Drake once plundered a mule train said to have been carrying 15 tons of gold—enough to build 30 Elizabethan warships. The glint of gold beneath the silt on the sea floor is the dream of many an underwater treasure hunter. These doubloons were recovered from the *Atocha*, a galleon lost near Cuba in a hurricane in 1622. She was heavy with gold and silver from Mexico.

AMERICA

The Spanish Main was first encountered by Columbus in 1492 while trying to find a sea passage to India and the East in pursuit of new trade routes.

WARDING OFF RIVALS

Single ships or small squadrons of ships were easy prey so, from 1543, the Spanish used two fleets to collect the treasure from the Spanish Main. One fleet would collect Mexican treasure, the other, Peruvian gold and silver. They would then meet and sail (about 100 ships in all) back to Spain. In retaliation, the English attacked and tried to colonize the ports and harbors from which the treasure ships sailed. In 1585 Drake led a fleet of 21 warships against the Spanish ports of Santo Domingo and Cartagena.

SPANISH GALLEON

Spanish ships loaded with treasure came under attack from privateers and pirates. In the course of the battles many ships sank beneath the waves. Many probably still lay undiscovered, filled with their precious cargo on the seabed. For the few who have found such ships, the rewards are enormous because the gold, silver, and jewels have continued to accumulate value over the intervening centuries. The Caribbean seas hold the secret of many a treasure ship and the balmy shallow waters make it the perfect environment for amateur and professional diver alike.

PIRATES!

Some Spanish soldiers joined up with groups of runaway slaves, deserters, and convicts, and together attacked the treasure ships for their own personal gain. These pirates lived by their own laws and they were often ruthless and bloody. Probably the most famous buccaneer is Sir Henry Morgan, who became Governor of Jamaica, and Blackbeard, the most famous pirate of all. By the mid 1700s governments no longer turned to privateering and established naval patrols in an effort to stamp out the pirate threat.

SPANISH SILVER

The riches of countries such as Bolivia were systematically stripped and shipped back to Spain. In mines such as the Cerro Silver mine (right) the native peoples were forced to work as slaves and were treated ruthlessly by their European masters.

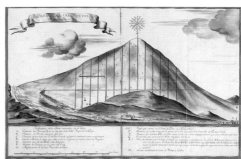

The *Royal George*

> "Toll for the brave
> The brave that are no more."
>
> *William Cowper*

The *Royal George* sank on August 29, 1782, 1.5 miles (2.5 km) off Spithead near Portsmouth, in front of a fleet of 30 to 40 ships. Weather conditions were calm at the time. What makes this shipwreck worse than the many others was that of the 1,200 on board, there were 300 women and 60 children. Of these, only one woman and one child are known to have survived.

In total, 900 people died, including Rear Admiral Richard Kempenfelt, head of the English fleet at that time. Witnesses say they heard a loud "crack" below deck, others say they heard nothing.

The Court Martial decided that, due to the rotten state of her timbers, part of the frame gave out when she leaned, or heeled, over. This decision was felt by some to cover up the officers' incompetence and carelessness. Vice Admiral Milbank said at the hearing that there wasn't a sound timber in her, even though she had been refitted in 1782.

LAMB OF GOD

Among the survivors were the plumber working below deck on a broken pipe and a seaman who was carried up the hatchway by in-rushing water. A young boy called Jack clung to a sheep and was rescued by a gentleman who later provided for him and called him Jack Lamb.

FINDING THE *ROYAL GEORGE*

In July 1783 there was a successful bid for funds to raise the *Royal George*. The government supplied two ships and stores, and the promise of a large sum of money to a man called Tracey if he could raise the ship. Tracey attached cables to the ship, making a cradle, which moved it for at least 30 ft. (10 m), but bad weather caused delays and the race against the spring tides defeated his efforts for that year. He applied to try again the following year but was refused permission.

THE *ROYAL GEORGE* BELL

From 1834-1836 the Deane brothers were to dive on the wreck of the *Royal George* using the copper-helmeted diving suit invented by John Deane. The story goes that while trying to save some horses from a fire, John Deane borrowed the helmet from a suit of armor. He secured to it the farm's failed water pipe and went into the smoke while a farmer slowly pumped air. Because of primitive diving techniques the most valuable items were salvaged first. These were the brass and iron guns and the ship's bell.

THE *ROYAL GEORGE* AT DOCK

The *Royal George* was 26 years old and the oldest "first rate" ship in the service. On her last cruise the *Royal George* had been taking on water and was ordered in to dock. However, after a strict survey by experts, the leak was discovered and repaired, so docking was avoided. On August 28, it was noticed that the pipe delivering fresh water, which was situated just below the water line, was broken. It was the effort to repair this pipe that caused her to sink.

A RUM DEAL

The most likely cause for her sinking started with a decision made by Admiral Kempenfelt to heel the ship to give access to the leaking freshwater pipe. When the men from the *Lark* unloaded tons of rum on the ship's low side, prior to stowing, she became so low that the slightest sea ripple entered the ship's lower gun-deck ports and she gradually began to sink. The carpenter, becoming aware of this, apparently asked the Lieutenant of the watch twice to right the ship. A sudden breeze blew and water rushed in to the lower ports. The workmen cried for the heeling to stop. The Lieutenant gave the order, but too late. The ship went down starboard side up, the water forcing out the air as she sank. Boats from the fleet, although quickly on the scene, were kept away by the whirlpool swirl. On touching the seabed she settled with her masts nearly upright.

THE RAFT OF THE MEDUSA

Theodore Gericault was to paint his masterpiece based on the events of 1816. He painted 15 survivors and several trapped corpses afloat on the raft. Two of the survivors posed for the picture. It took 10 months to do the preliminary sketches and a further eight to make the painting. He never quite recovered from the despair he felt after completing this painting and in 1824 died after a long illness.

The painting was originally listed under another title: *Scene of Shipwreck*. This may have been because its true title was politically sensitive at a time when there was still much bad feeling between the Monarchists and the Republicans.

CANNIBALISM

Events on the raft quickly deteriorated. The men mutinied and fighting broke out. Some were killed before they expired from thirst and hunger, some committed suicide. With so much dead flesh, the survivors, forced by hunger, turned to cannibalism. Amazingly, after 52 days the wreck was finally discovered with four men still alive. A total of 155 people died.

RAFT AND BOATS

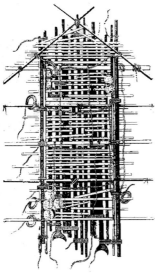

On paper (right) the raft would carry 200 people plus provisions. The ship's boats would tow the raft. It was badly planned and crudely constructed, any buoyancy being provided by the frame to which timbers were fixed and planks nailed. After three days the weather changed and the *Medusa* started to break up. De Chaumarey left with all the favored, Monarchist passengers in the boats, along with their provisions. The raft could only manage about 160 people, consisting mainly of soldiers who were submerged up to their waists in water. Their only provisions were six barrels of wine and two barrels of water. The remaining 60 or so, including women and children, were left to perish on board the *Medusa*.

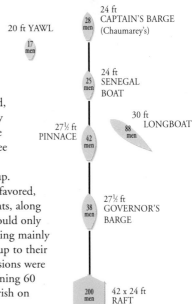

20 ft YAWL — 17 men

24 ft CAPTAIN'S BARGE (Chaumarey's) — 28 men

24 ft SENEGAL BOAT — 25 men

27½ ft PINNACE — 42 men

30 ft LONGBOAT — 88 men

27½ ft GOVERNOR'S BARGE — 38 men

42 x 24 ft RAFT — 200 men

The *Medusa*

In 1816 a French frigate, *Medusa,* was in a squadron of four ships that set sail for Senegal in West Africa. This English colony was being handed back to the French, so the *Medusa* was carrying all kinds of professional people for the task ahead. The passengers and crews of the four ships consisted of an uneasy mix of both Republicans and Monarchists. In charge was the captain of the *Medusa*, de Chaumarey, a Monarchist who won his command by favor from King Louis XVIII despite the fact that he had not sailed for 25 years. At this time the waters off the African coast were poorly charted and the Ministry warned de Chaumarey of a particularly dangerous sand bank, the Arguin Bank, telling him to steer well clear even though this would make the journey longer. During the voyage de Chaumarey was persuaded by his crew to go the shortest and most dangerous route. By this time the rest of the convoy had left the *Medusa,* following Ministry guidelines to take the safest route. On July 2, the *Medusa* ran aground on the sand bank. Confusion and indecision set in. Some suggested ferrying people ashore, others thought that if the ship were light enough it could be sailed. One passenger suggested making a raft since there were only six boats. The captain decided on the raft.

Emperor Napoleon was one of the most powerful leaders of modern history. His rule, however, saw terrible conflict between rival factions in his native France. It was his defeat at the Battle of Waterloo that saw the end to French domination of Europe, and England handed back Senegal as part of the peace settlement.

A MODERN *MEDUSA*

A French film reenacting the events aboard the *Medusa* was as dramatic as the real event. The director tried to kill himself in front of the French Cultural Minister in order to draw attention to the fact that its release had been deliberately delayed.

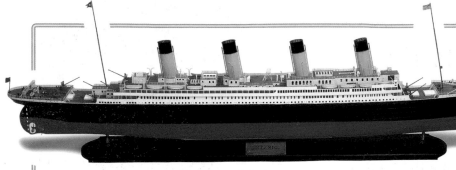

THE NEWS SPREADS

Only 705 people from the 2,228 on board survived. Those that made it into the lifeboats were eventually picked up by the *Carpathia,* which sailed as fast as she could to the scene of the wreck. She was, however, too late for those who quickly perished in the ice-cold water. Although distress calls were sent by wireless, by Morse lamp, and by rockets from the stricken ship, a ship in the distance never answered her calls. Some thought the mystery ship was the S.S. *Californian,* which had earlier sent an urgent ice warning to the *Titanic.* The *Titanic's* wireless operator, busy with passenger telegrams, apparently told the sender to "shut up," later apologizing and asking for the message to be repeated, but without success.

THE SINKING OF THE *TITANIC*

On Sunday, April 14, 1912, about 350 miles (565 km) southeast of Newfoundland and traveling at approximately 20 knots, the *Titanic* hit an iceberg. It was a dark night, with a slight mist and no moonlight. Several messages had been received warning of heavy pack-ice, field ice, and a great number of icebergs. An earlier message had been received by the Captain and noted and there was a lookout, but in trying to avoid a collision the *Titanic* turned hard to starboard and the hull below the waterline was damaged. She took 2 hours and 40 minutes to sink. The ship's orchestra apparently played throughout.

The *Titanic*

Perhaps the most famous shipwreck of all time is that of the *Titanic*. The White Star Line built the *Titanic* and her sister ship, the *Olympic*, to be the biggest, best, and safest passenger vessels afloat. It took 11,300 Harland & Wolff shipyard workers 26 months to build the *Titanic*. She was spacious, luxurious, and supposedly unsinkable and had a service speed of 21 knots.

TITANIC LEAVING SOUTHAMPTON HARBOR

The *Titanic* began her maiden voyage from Southampton on April 10, 1912 sailing for New York. Four days later, this magnificent ship was on the ocean floor.

The communication system was the most powerful ever used on a merchant vessel, and at night it was possible to reach a range of up to 2,000 miles. The *Titanic* had a double bottom construction and 16 watertight compartments of which any two could be flooded without affecting the buoyancy of the ship, thus improving safety.

TITANIC SURVIVORS

Of the 2,228 people on board there were only enough lifeboats for 1,178. British government regulations worked on cubic footage and not the number of passengers. In fact, there were 20 lifeboats on board the *Titanic,* which exceeded government guidelines by 12 percent. Original plans had called for 48 lifeboats. The first lifeboats lowered were not even full, such was the belief that the ship wouldn't sink. The boats should have taken 53 percent of those on board instead of the 32 percent who actually survived.

ONE OF THE MANY TRAGIC TALES

With 1,500 people left aboard and one lifeboat capable of carrying 47 people, the crew locked arms around the boat and told women and children to board. Of those left was Michel Navratil and his two sons whom he had kidnapped from his wife, hoping to make a new start in America. The last time he saw them was when he handed Michel and Edmond over to the crew.

TITANIC – THE MOVIE

In 1997 the American film director James Cameron made a film of the *Titanic* story. This epic film, centering on the fate of two star-crossed lovers who were passengers on the ship, has proved to be one of the most successful films of all time, breaking box office records around the world. The special effects were based on evidence gathered from the many dives on the shipwreck.

TITANIC MODEL

This model of the *Titanic* shows the two main parts of the wrecked hull, and how she lies on the seabed today.

ILLUSTRATION

As Jack Thayer watched the *Titanic* sink from one of the lifeboats, he drew the event unfolding before him. For many years the sketch of the hull breaking in two was not believed.

The *Titanic*

The British inquiry concluded that the bottom of the starboard side of the vessel, about 10 ft. (3 m) above the level of the keel, had been damaged by the iceberg and that the damage reached about 300 ft. (100 m), taking less than 10 seconds to occur given a speed of 20 knots. As water spilled over the bulkheads the stern gradually rose out of the water until, when it reached an angle of about 60 degrees, it sank with lights still ablaze. Immediate plans were made to locate the wreck but it lay 2.5 miles (4.5 km) beneath the surface and technology at the time could not respond to the challenge. Little more was heard until 1958 when a film entitled *A Night to Remember* was made. Nearly thirty years later, in 1985, a joint French and American team discovered the Titanic, seeing images of the ship transmitted from underwater video cameras. The ship lay in two pieces, ripped apart midships. Exploration was difficult at such extreme depths, but the *Titanic*'s mystery nevertheless encouraged the scientists to find new ways of visiting the wreck.

EXPLORING THE *TITANIC*

Nadir is the French government's undersea exploration agency survey ship. It has worked with an American company, RMS *Titanic* Inc., to explore the wreck. *Nautile* is a three-man submersible with robotic arms that has been operating up to 19,600 ft. (6,000 m) deep, searching the wreck, and sending information back to the mother ship, *Nadir*. It takes one and a half hours to descend to the seabed and, because of the enormous pressure from the sea at this depth, *Nautile*'s core is titanium. Attached to *Nautile* is Robin, a video camera, which can swim away, entering those areas the submersible cannot.

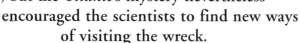

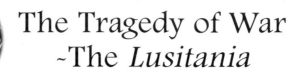

The Tragedy of War
~The *Lusitania*

TRUE OR FALSE?

Photographs of victims and detailed sketches filled the newspapers and magazines; however pictures such as this one were not real but were recreated for propaganda purposes. The *Lusitania*'s name on the boat in this picture is far too large.

On May 7, 1915, a few kilometers off the Old Head of Kinsale on the southern coast of Ireland, the *Lusitania* was sunk. It was a warm spring day and picnickers on the nearby coast watched in horror as the ship was hit by a torpedo on the starboard side. A large explosion followed a few seconds later. In just 18 minutes she had sunk with the loss of 1,195 passengers and crew. Of those dead, 123 were Americans. Only 764 survived. The sinking shocked the world; surely no sailors of any civilized nation would sink an unarmed passenger liner! Survivors recall two explosions, but records show that the German U-boat, *U-20*, fired only one torpedo. For years there was speculation that the *Lusitania* was not an innocent passenger liner as the British would have everyone believe. Some claimed she was carrying high explosives purchased in America for use by the British army in France. Rumor had it that the British wanted the ship sunk so that America would join the Allied forces in the war against Germany.

DOOMED TO DIE

With an inexperienced crew, the absence of any passenger lifeboat drill and the speed at which the *Lusitania* was sinking, the launching of the lifeboats was almost impossible. With the ship listing hard to port, most of the boats on this side were smashed and the occupants tumbled into the sea. Only one or two boats made it to sea without damage.

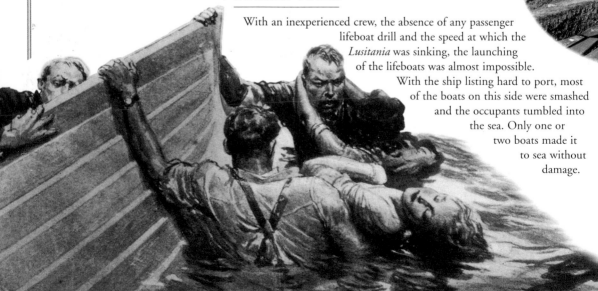

The Sinking of the Lusitania.
May 7th 1915.

THE PROPAGANDA WAR

The sinking of the ship generated a great deal of publicity that the British government used as propaganda. Endless posters and cartoons depicting the sinking were produced, as well as press releases, copies of photographs, written scripts for slide shows and articles for magazines. British military authorities noticed a marked increase in enlistments. It was a highly successful campaign and generated more support for the Allied cause than any number of political speeches.

THE MASS FUNERAL

Hundreds of bodies were washed up or brought ashore many days after the sinking. The dead were placed in coffins in the Cunard yard while British soldiers dug mass graves in a cemetery outside Queenstown. Many passengers had drowned because their life belts were too loose or were upside down and many more died because they didn't have enough time to get to their life belts. It was common practice in wartime for all crew and passengers to wear life belts when they entered a danger zone, but the captain had not instructed them to do so. The inquests that followed failed to ask many relevant questions. The inquiry by the Board of Trade found Germany guilty, absolving Cunard and the Royal Navy of any blame.

RAISING THE *LUSITANIA*

In the 1930s Jim Jarret was the first diver to stand on the wreck of the *Lusitania*. Wearing heavy and clumsy diving gear, and with ineffective lighting, he thought the ship was lying on her port side. It was 25 years later when John Light, with the aid of scuba gear and better lighting, confirmed that the ship was in fact lying on her starboard side with a gigantic hole in the ship's port side. Because the fractured steel plate was bent outward, he thought it a sure sign that there had been an internal explosion of tremendous force. This reinforced suspicions that the U-boat attack detonated illegal explosives.

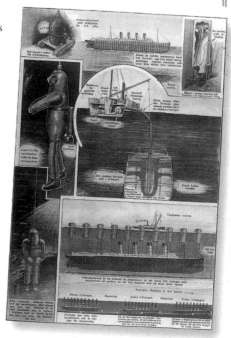

THE GRAND DAME OF THE SEA

The lavishly appointed liner was thought to be unsinkable, just like the *Titanic* before her, and had been built to the latest safety standards just three years earlier.

A NARROW ESCAPE

Fourteen-year-old Linda Morgan had a narrow escape. Reports state that she was thrown by the impact from Cabin 52 on the *Andrea Doria* onto the deck of the *Stockholm*. She survived along with her mother, but her stepfather, Camille Cianfarra, foreign correspondent of the *New York Times*, was killed together with her eight-year-old stepsister. In all, 51 people died, 46 on the *Andrea Doria* and five on the *Stockholm*. Many were killed by the impact as the bow of the *Stockholm* tore into cabins as passengers were preparing for bed.

The *Andrea Doria*

One of the biggest news stories of 1956 was the sinking of the *Andrea Doria*. The Italian luxury liner was sailing towards New York on July 25, 1956, carrying 1,706 passengers and crew on her 51st transatlantic crossing. The liner was due to make New York by 9 A.M. the following morning, but she hit fog off the Nantucket coast and, by evening, visibility was reduced to under 2/3 of a mile (1 km). The Captain, Pietro Calamai, should have slowed the ship in such conditions, but it appeared that he was anxious to make port on time because the ship's speed reduced only a fraction from the maximum 23 knots. Also making its way through the fog that night, outward bound from New York, was a passenger liner the *Stockholm,* belonging to the Swedish American line. The *Stockholm* carried 747 passengers and crew. They were both headed on a fateful collision course.

ANDREA DORIA

The *Andrea Doria* was named after the 16th-century Italian Admiral depicted on this medal. His bronze statue adorned the first class lounge, and was the first artifact to be recovered by a salvage team in 1964.

S.O.S.

Mrs. Dickson, a passenger on the *Andrea Doria,* was on the dance floor when the two ships collided. She recalls seeing a large shower of sparks and hearing shrieking metal, then the dance floor tilting at a crazy angle. Seawater rushed into the damaged starboard side causing the ship to list heavily.

There was an immediate scramble for the lifeboats as passengers attempted to save themselves. The *Stockholm* managed to secure watertight compartments and rescue passengers from the *Andrea Doria.*

The *Andrea Doria* slowly slipped under the waves as the first news reporters arrived, flying over the scene and giving an eyewitness account of the ship's last moments.

COLLISION COURSE

10:40 p.m. The *Andrea Doria* picks up the *Stockholm* on its radar at a range of 27 miles (10½ km).

10:50 p.m. The *Stockholm* changes course.

11:05 p.m. The *Andrea Doria* changes course. The ships are now closing on each other.

11:07 p.m. The *Stockholm* steers 20 degrees to starboard and the *Andrea Doria* takes emergency action, turning to port to avoid the other ship bearing down on her. The *Stockholm* turns to starboard in a final desperate avoiding action.

11:10 p.m. The reinforced ice-breaking bow of the *Stockholm* ploughs into the starboard side of the *Andrea Doria.* The damage is severe.

11:20 p.m. Captain Calamai sends the first S.O.S. message. He knows the *Andrea Doria* is doomed.

02:00 a.m The liner *Ile de France* is the first ship to answer the S.O.S. and rescues 753 passengers.

05:30 a.m. The captain and senior officers are the last to leave the stricken vessel.

10:09 a.m. The *Andrea Doria* slips under the waves.

Environmental Disasters

SEA EMPRESS

The oil tanker *Sea Empress* ran aground in southwest Wales on February 5, 1996. Bad weather conditions made the ship's rescue all the more difficult and it is estimated that 72,000 tons of crude oil were lost. Eventually the ship was towed to Belfast. The cleanup operation was put into action very quickly.

Modern shipwrecks can have a disastrous effect on the marine environment. Today's supertankers carry thousands of tons of crude oil ready for refining into oil-based products such as gasoline. Today, these dangers are seen to outweigh the threat posed to human life by sinking ships. Cargo ships, such as supertankers, often only carry a handful of crew, and safety at sea is greatly improved thanks to such factors as accurate satellite navigation systems, the availability of detailed charts, and the sheer size of ships, which are able to ride out rough weather. However, when something goes wrong, it does so on a huge scale and human error is often to blame. Scientists have learned how to respond rapidly and effectively to disasters, such as oil spills, and are quickly able to minimize the damage that ensues.

THE *EXXON VALDEZ*

In 1989 the *Exxon Valdez* ran aground at Prince William Sound, in Alaska, dumping 267,000 barrels of oil (11 million gallons) over approximately 10,000 square miles (25,000 square km). Its effect on the ecosystem was severe and made more so because the accident happened in cold water. This prolongs the life of toxins and will affect wildlife species for generations. At the time, it was the largest oil spill ever in the United States.

WILDLIFE IN DANGER

In the *Exxon Valdez* disaster, thousands
of seabirds, otters, fish, and kelp were killed
as well as 16 whales and 147 bald eagles.

CLEANUP

The cleanup operation after the *Exxon Valdez*
disaster has been heavily criticized for its mismanagement because
damaging hydrocarbons were permitted to seep into the earth.
Alternatively, the cleanup after the *Sea Empress* disaster has been cited as
one of the most successful. Oil was recovered from the sea in sheltered
areas and was taken to the open sea where it was broken down with
chemicals. The oil coating the beaches was treated with high-pressure hoses
and scrapers. For the rocky areas, they used absorbent materials. The
inaccessible areas were left to the natural cleaning power of the sea.

THE *AMOCO CADIZ*

During a storm in 1978, the American supertanker *Amoco
Cadiz,* filled with 223,000 tons of crude oil, ran aground off
the Brittany coast discharging its entire load into the Atlantic
Ocean. Some 130 beaches were coated in the oil and over
30,000 seabirds died along with millions of crabs, lobsters, and
other fish, destroying the livelihoods of many local people.
Standard Oil of Indiana was found guilty of negligence
and failure to train the ship's crew. In 1988,
$85 million in damages was awarded
to the Breton communities (some
400,000 people) affected
by the disaster.

EXXON VALDEZ

Human Disasters

THE *ESTONIA'S* LIFE RAFTS

Passengers of the *Estonia* struggled to get to the open decks as the ship rolled over. They scrambled onto the upturned hull where they were washed off by the waves. Within 50 minutes the ship sank. Only 137 passengers survived. Many were trapped and never made it into the 40 life rafts that floated, mostly empty, on the freezing seas.

*T*ragedies at sea resulting in terrible loss of life are still commonplace today despite all the advances in ship technology and safety measures. Often, human error is to blame, with either crew negligence or passenger ignorance resulting in disaster. Those that result in the loss of large numbers of people are ferry ships, which often operate – and sink – in shallow coastal waters. Sometimes they occur in inland waters, such as the ferry MV *Bukoba*, which sank in Lake Victoria, Tanzania, in 1996 with huge loss of life. The ferry was heavily overcrowded, which may have been a factor in the capsizing. The following year about 180 passengers drowned when a Haitian ferry sank just about 1,000 feet from shore. It was not known how many were on board, and an unknown number swam safely to shore.

THE *HERALD OF FREE ENTERPRISE*

On March 6, 1987 the *Herald of Free Enterprise* left Zeebrugge harbor in Belgium with approximately 500 passengers and 80 crew. Only 20 minutes into the journey and 1.5 miles (2.5 km) from shore, the vessel capsized in freezing cold water. It took just 60 seconds to turn over. Eleven hundred tons of haulage, cars, and trucks shifted portside along with the passengers and anything that wasn't fastened down. There wasn't even time for a Mayday call. Nearly 200 lives were lost. A dredger saw the capsize and immediately raised the alarm, and within 30 minutes salvage ships, tugboats, and a helicopter were on the scene.

THE *ESTONIA* FERRY DISASTER

On September 27, 1994 the ferry *Estonia* sailed from Estonia to Stockholm carrying 989 passengers. About halfway into its journey across the Baltic, and in heavy seas with 20 ft. (6 m) high waves the ferry's huge steel bow door was torn from its hinges by the force of the sea (recovered later as shown). The ship listed to one side, allowing seawater to pour into the lower decks. The crew, unsure as to what had happened, maneuvered the *Estonia* sideways hoping the wind and waves would push her back onto an even keel. It had the opposite effect, allowing 20 tons of water per second to enter the stricken vessel.

GREENPEACE SINKING

The trawler *Sir William Hardy* was purchased by the environmental group "Greenpeace," with help from the World Wildlife Fund, for its campaign to protect whales in the North Atlantic. Renamed *Rainbow Warrior*, she was painted in rainbow colors with a dove of peace carrying an olive branch on the bow. Greenpeace used her in many protests against activities that posed a threat to the environment, including campaigning against the dumping of nuclear and toxic waste by a number of countries. In 1985 the *Rainbow Warrior* arrived in Auckland to arrange a peaceful antinuclear demonstration. While in the harbor, French secret agents bombed and sank the vessel, killing a Greenpeace photographer. The French government, after two years of arbitration, paid $8.159 million in compensation.

A FISHY HOME

It was decided to bury the *Rainbow Warrior* at sea in Matauri Bay in New Zealand with a full Maori ceremony on December 12, 1987. The wreck, sunk in deep, clear waters, has become an artificial reef with an abundance of life and is visited by many divers. In 1989 the new *Rainbow Warrior*, another North Sea Trawler, was launched and includes an educational theater and workshop.

THE *HERALD OF FREE ENTERPRISE* RESCUE OPERATION

This rescue operation was well-organized and efficient, and within 15 minutes specialist teams were at the ready in hospitals. Later on, the *Herald of Free Enterprise* was successfully raised and an investigation carried out into the cause of the disaster. It was found that the doors of the car deck had been left open, allowing water to rush onto the lower deck, destabilizing the vessel.

Gazetteer

The world's oceans are littered with thousands of wrecked ships. Even today, the fishing fleets of every nation regularly lose ships at sea, but these daily tragedies never make it into the news headlines. The majority of ships that founder at sea will never be discovered, and the causes will never be known. The relentless movement of the waves and the corrosive power of salt water quickly reduce sunken ships until nothing recognizable remains. Occasionally, however, divers discover wrecks and retrieve a little piece of history before it is consumed forever beneath the waves. This map shows the locations of the wrecks described in this book.

THE *EXXON VALDEZ*

The Exxon Valdez *runs aground in Alaska.*

THE SPANISH ARMADA

Treasures from the Girona.

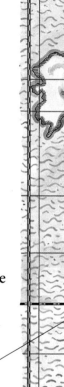

THE *ANDREA DORIA*

Named after the 16th-century Italian Admiral depicted on this medal.

THE *TITANIC*

The Titanic *sinks on her maiden voyage.*

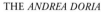

TREASURE

Doubloons recovered from the Atocha.

30

THE *LUSITANIA*

It took just 18 minutes
for the Lusitania
to sink.

THE *SEA EMPRESS*

It is estimated that
72,000 tons of
oil were lost.

THE *MARY ROSE*

Flagship of
Henry VIII's fleet.

THE *ESTONIA*
FERRY DISASTER

Sank en route
to Stockholm.

THE *HERALD
OF FREE
ENTERPRISE*

Nearly 200
lives were lost.

THE *ROYAL
GEORGE*

Sank off
Spithead near
Portsmouth.

THE *SERCE
LIMANI*

Sank off
the southern
coast of Turkey.

THE *MEDUSA*

Theodore Gericault's masterpiece,
The Raft of the Medusa.

THE *AMOCO CADIZ*

223,000 tons of crude oil were
discharged into the Atlantic Ocean.

THE *RAINBOW
WARRIOR*

French secret agents
bomb and sink the
Rainbow Warrior.

STORIES OF SURVIVAL

The wedding. The Indonesian ferry *Gurita* sank in a storm off the coast of Malaysia in January 1996. More than 150 people were lost, but among the 47 survivors were Londoner Steve Nicholson, and his girlfriend Caroline Harrison. Harrison overcame her fear of the sea to take the ferry that night but was plunged into the sea as the ferry sank. Together they kept afloat for over 12 hours and, not knowing whether they would survive, Nicholson proposed marriage. Caroline Harrison accepted.

Shark alert. New Yorker Margaret Crotty was also a passenger on the *Gurita*. When the ferry sank, Crotty jumped into the sea. She grabbed hold of a rubber life raft but was pushed off by passengers who feared it might capsize. Crotty removed her trousers, knotted the legs and trapped air into them creating a balloon that helped her stay afloat for 16 hours before finally reaching land. Her greatest fear was that she had cut her leg getting off the ferry and that hungry sharks might be attracted by the blood.

Saved by a bucket. In 1993 the ferry *Neptune* sank in a storm off the coast of Haiti. It was thought that about 2,000 passengers were on board, of which only 285 survived. The captain, Benjamin St. Clair, told how the passengers panicked when the ferry began to roll in the heavy seas, rushing from one side to the other. One survivor hugged a bag of charcoal for 15 hours after being swept into the sea. A woman survived by hanging onto a small white bucket. The ship carried no lifeboats, jackets, radios or other emergency equipment.

Heroic volunteers. The sailing ship *Heroine* foundered in a storm off the Dorset coast in 1852. Its fate could be seen from the nearby shore and five volunteers decided to row out to the stricken ship. Crowds cheered as they launched their boat, but after a few minutes the boat was smashed back onto the breakwater and four of the five drowned. Meanwhile the crew and passengers of the *Heroine* were approaching shore in two of the ship's boats. A survivor swam ashore with a rope between his teeth and everyone was hauled to safety.

ACKNOWLEDGMENTS

We would like to thank Graham Rich, Rosalind Beckman, and Elizabeth Wiggans for their assistance and David Hobbs for his map of the world.
First edition for the United States, Canada, and Philippines published by Barron's Educational Series, Inc., 1999
First published in Great Britain in 1999 by *ticktock* Publishing Ltd., The Office, The Square, Hadlow, Kent, TN11 0DD, United Kingdom
Copyright © 1999 ticktock Publishing Ltd. American edition Copyright © 1999 Barron's Educational Series, Inc.

All inquiries should be addressed to: Barron's Educational Series, Inc., 250 Wireless Boulevard, Hauppauge, New York 11788. http://www.barronseduc.com
Library of Congress Catalog Card No. 98-74957
International Standard Book Number 0-7641-0646-5

Picture research by Image Select.
Printed in Hong Kong.
987654321

Picture Credits
t=top, b=bottom, c=center, l=left, r=right, OFC=outside front cover, OBC=outside back cover, IFC=inside front cover

AKG: IFC, 5cr, 9br, 10tl, 11br, 12bl & 32ct, 17tr. Ann Ronan Picture Library: 2cl, 2cb, 2tl. Cephas Picture Library/Mick Rock: 15br. Chris Fairclough Colour Library: 14tl. Colorific: 2/3t, 8bl, 21tr, 21cr, 26/27 (main pic) & 30ct. Corbis: 24tl, 24bl, 24cr, 24br, 25c, 25tr & 30cl. Draeger Limited: 3br. e.t. archive: 13br, 18cl & OFC. FPG International: 22tl. Giraudon: 16/17t & 31bl. Glasgow Museums: The Stirling Maxwell Collection, Pollok House: 10/11b. Hulton Getty: 19c, 18/19c & OFC, 22/23c. Illustrated London News: 20bl. Institute of Nautical Archaeology: 6tl, 6bl & 31crb, 7tl, 6/7c, 7br. John Eaton and Charles Haas: 19br. Mary Evans Picture Library: 13tr, 22bl & OBC, 22/23t & 30tr & OBC, 23br. Mary Rose Trust: 8tl & 31ctr, 8br, 8/9c. National Maritime Museum: 11tr, 12/13c & OFC, 14/15c, 14bl, 15tr & 31crc & OBC, 16cl, 18tl & 30bl, 20/21c. Planet Earth: OFC (diver), 2/3c, 5cb, 12tl & 30br & OFC. Rex Features: 4/5t, 26tl & 31ctl, 26/27t, 27tr, 27cr & 31cb, 28cr & 31crt, 28tl, 28bl & 31tr, 28/29t & 31br, 29br. Spectrum Colour Library: 29cr. Telegraph Colour Library: 4b, 4tl, 9tr. The Kobal Collection: 20tl, 20ct. The Stock Market: 4/5 (main pic). Trustees of the National Museums and Galleries of Northern Ireland: 10bl & 30tr & OBC, 10c. Ulster Folk and Transport Museum: 19tr. Utopia Productions: 17br.

Every effort has been made to trace the copyright holders and we apologize in advance for any unintentional omissions.
We would be pleased to insert the appropriate acknowledgment in any subsequent edition of this publication.

BARRON'S